A Quiet PLACE

A Quiet PLACE

How Daily Prayer Can
Change Your Life

FR. JOHN BARTUNEK

BEACON

Unless otherwise noted, Scripture passages have been taken from the
Revised Standard Version, Catholic Edition. Copyright © 1946, 1952, 1971 by
the Division of Christian Education of the National Council of Churches
of Christ in the USA. Used by permission. All rights reserved.

Quotes are taken from the English translation of the *Catechism of the
Catholic Church* for the United States of America (indicated as *CCC*), 2nd
edition. Copyright © 1997 by United States Catholic Conference—Libreria
Editrice Vaticana.

Design by Ashley Wirfel

ISBN 978-1-929266-29-6 (softcover)

Library of Congress Cataloging-in-Publication Data
Names: Bartunek, John, author.
Title: A quiet place : how daily prayer can change your life / John
Bartunek, LC, SThD.
Description: North Palm Beach : Beacon Publishing, 2017.
Identifiers: LCCN 2017020564 | ISBN 9781929266296 (softcover)
Subjects: LCSH: Prayer—Christianity. | Catholic Church—Doctrines.
Classification: LCC BV210.3 .B373 2017 | DDC
248.3/2—dc23

Dynamic Catholic® and Be Bold. Be Catholic.® and The Best Version of
Yourself® are registered trademarks of The Dynamic Catholic Institute.

For more information on this title or other books and CDs available
through the Dynamic Catholic Book Program,
please visit www.DynamicCatholic.com.

The Dynamic Catholic Institute
5081 Olympic Blvd • Erlanger • Kentucky • 41018
Phone: 1–859–980–7900
Email: info@DynamicCatholic.com

Second printing, December 2017

Printed in the United States of America

TABLE *of* CONTENTS

INTRODUCTION

When we were in kindergarten, we learned the alphabet. Since then, we have learned to read and write and have done an awful lot of it. We are certainly better readers and writers now than we were when we first learned the alphabet.

When we were getting ready for our first Communion, someone taught us to pray, or at least to say some prayers. Since then, has our prayer life grown and expanded the way it was meant to, the way our reading and writing grew and expanded after learning the alphabet? Is it still growing and expanding?

If you have a sense that somewhere along the line your prayer life stopped growing, or that it never really got much of a start in the first place, you need this book. You need to jump-start your prayer life.

Prayer is so much more than just "saying your prayers." Prayer is a spiritual adventure. It brings interior depth and meaning that can come from nowhere else—*absolutely nowhere else.*

If you feel a need or desire for greater spiritual depth, or even a slight suspicion that something is missing in your life, spiritually speaking, then I can guarantee that now is the right time for *A Quiet Place.* Keep reading, and let the adventure begin.

ONE
Why Pray?

Imagine you have an acorn in the palm of your left hand and a stone the same size and shape as an acorn in your right hand. Look at these items: They look similar, feel similar, and weigh almost the same. What's the difference between them?

If you plant one of them in the right conditions, it will begin to put out shoots and roots and start to grow. And, once again given the right conditions, that growth will continue unabated for perhaps two centuries. A gorgeous oak tree will emerge from the acorn, giving beauty and fruitfulness to the world for hundreds of years.

But if you plant the stone in the same soil, under the same conditions, nothing will happen. The stone will just stay a stone. It will not sprout, or grow, or beautify the landscape, or give food and shelter and shade to people and animals and birds for centuries.

The acorn bears within itself the mysterious force of *life*. It is a seed—small, vulnerable, but full of magnificent potential. All it needs in order to fulfill this potential are the right conditions: good soil, water, sunlight, and a healthy climate.

The stone, on the other hand, is inanimate. It is dead

matter. It has no life, no potential to grow and organically develop into something magnificent and wonderful.

STONY SPIRITS

Before we were baptized, our souls were like that stone. Original sin had cut us off from grace, the life of God that alone can lead us to fulfillment as human beings. God created human beings in his own image and likeness; he created us to live in communion with him. That communion of life with God, in whom alone we can find lasting happiness, is what we mean by the word *grace.*

But, tempted by the devil, our first parents rebelled against God's plan for their lives. And so they freely cut themselves and all their descendants off from God's grace. The life, the potential for the spiritual growth and fruitfulness that can only come from living in communion with God, was drained from our spirits. Instead of the spiritual acorns that we were created to be, we became stones, spiritually speaking.

God in his goodness didn't abandon us there. He reached out to Adam and Eve, and he initiated a plan of salvation that would gradually unfold throughout the entire history of humanity. The central piece in that plan was his Incarnation. God didn't want to save us from afar. In Jesus Christ, God actually entered this fallen human race, this world of spiritual stones. He became one of us and restored the life of grace. When he shed his own blood by dying on the cross on the first Good Friday, his very own divine life was poured out upon the earth. Grace returned.

Since then, it has been his Church's mission to spread this grace into every human heart, and to create the right conditions for the seed of divine life that grace brings to put out its shoots and roots, to grow and flourish and bear spiritual fruit for this fallen world. That is what we call redemption, and it is why Jesus Christ is known as the Savior and Redeemer.

As individuals, we begin to experience this redemption when we are baptized. Baptism is the way Jesus invented for restoring the life of grace after original sin. Through this sacrament, the spiritual stone within us is transformed into an acorn. We are brought back into communion with God, and given the hope of growing into the only form of spiritual maturity that can bring us fulfillment.

OUR SPIRITUAL DNA

When grace takes root in a soul and grows to maturity, it produces what the Bible calls the "fruit of the Holy Spirit": love, joy, peace, patience, kindness, generosity, faithfulness, gentleness, and self-control (see Galatians 5:22). Just as acorns given the right conditions grow into magnificent oak trees that produce more acorns, so the spiritual seed of grace planted in our hearts and given the right conditions will grow and produce its own fruits. This gives our lives the meaning we were created to find, the meaning we yearn for and search for in so many mistaken places. Since grace is the seed of divine life within us, as it grows, it makes us more and more like God, restoring the image and likeness of God in which we were created, but which was damaged by original sin.

The actual life force at work in grace is mysterious. We can't understand it completely. But we do know some things. For instance, it brings the presence of God's own Holy Spirit within us. And the Holy Spirit enriches us with spiritual gifts that open up new levels of experience and a new degree of life intensity.

You have probably heard about some of these gifts: wisdom, understanding, knowledge, piety, fortitude, fear of the Lord, and counsel. Faith, hope, and Christlike love are also among God's gifts to a baptized person. They are not just feelings we have or actions we perform; they are spiritual forces present and active within us through grace. All these gifts naturally tend to stimulate the development of our true identity. They impel us, in a sense, toward the amazing dream that God has for each one of our lives.

This is what is so attractive, so mysteriously inspiring, about the lives of the saints. They are our older brothers and sisters in Christ, in whose lives grace truly flourished. They found and fulfilled their most genuine identity by living in communion with God, by living a real, unique, and dynamic relationship with him. They are the spiritual oak trees that fully show forth the magnificence of authentic human greatness and beautify the landscape of human history.

Mother Teresa of Calcutta, Francis of Assisi, Mary Magdalene, Augustine, Catherine of Siena, John Paul II . . . none of them started out as saints. But God's grace entered their lives, purified them of their brokenness and sin, and allowed them to flourish. The same grace that worked wonders in them is at work, like a seed waiting to grow and flourish, in every baptized soul—including yours.

GOOD SOIL FOR SPIRITUAL GROWTH

Love, joy, peace, patience, kindness, generosity, faithfulness, gentleness, self-control; wisdom, understanding, knowledge, piety, fear of the Lord, fortitude, counsel; faith, hope, Christ-like love—these are the ingredients of lasting happiness. They aren't meant to be the exclusive property of extraordinary saints. They are meant to enrich and shine out in every single one of us. These are the spiritual qualities that make life worth living, that produce healthy family life, that over-flow into the forging of a strong and creative culture. They are what we feel *called* to live, but constantly find ourselves falling short of living. Why is that?

If the right conditions for an acorn to become an oak tree are good soil, water, sunlight, and a healthy climate, what are the right conditions for the seed of grace to produce spiritual maturity? What makes it possible for this seed to grow, flourish, and yield its marvelous fruit?

One essential element is a life of prayer. In a sense, prayer is the soil in which grace can grow. The other sacraments (the Eucharist, confession, marriage, and so on) are like the water and the sunlight. Moral integrity and virtue are like the good climate. But the soil, the very ground that enables our spiritual potential to quicken, unfold, mature, and thrive, from the beginning of our spiritual journey until its very end, is prayer. If we want to experience in our own lives, ever more abundantly, the gifts and fruits of the Holy Spirit, and if we want to contribute through them to our loved ones and to the world around us, we simply must develop a life of prayer.

And we can. Really. Every single one of us can become an amazing pray-er. It doesn't take any special talent or genetic propensity. There is only one requirement, and it's something not even God can do for us: We simply have to be willing to try.

A GUY IN CHICAGO

I met a man in Chicago a few years ago, a Catholic man, married with two or three children. He had started his own business, and it was doing well. He had maybe a couple hundred employees. We got to talking about prayer and the spiritual life. He was using one of my books for his daily prayer time, and I asked him when he had started the spiritual discipline of praying every day. He paused for a second, then told me what had happened.

During the years when he was starting his business, he put in long hours and struggled to get by. Those were also the years when his children were still young, grade-school age. He wasn't spending much time with them, or with his wife; his business venture was taking up all his bandwidth. He would still go to Mass on Sundays, but that was the extent of his spiritual life.

After he'd spent years working at that breakneck pace, his business started to thrive. He finally began to find more time for his wife and his kids. But he was surprised when his attempts to reconnect with them came up dry. He kept trying. But somehow it wasn't working. His wife seemed like a stranger. His kids didn't seem to want him involved in their world. On the outside, the family was healthy and happy. But on the inside, he felt that his vision of what being a husband and a dad should be was unattainable. He didn't know what to do.

Gradually he became discouraged, and refocused his energy on his business. He remained on civil and generally pleasant terms with his wife and children, but he found more immediate gratification in his work, where he felt he could really make a difference and see tangible results. He reached a modus vivendi in which he kept providing for his family and loving them as much as they would let him (so it seemed to him). But his creative juices flowed at work, and his heart was more alive there. In the back of his mind he was worried, but he just kept the worry there and focused his attention on what he knew he was good at.

One weekend he was having breakfast with his wife, and out of the blue (so it seemed to him), she told him that she didn't know if she could continue the way things were. She felt alone and unappreciated. The kids (now adolescents) were having all kinds of issues. And although he provided for the family materially, he wasn't really present for any of them. That wasn't what she wanted. That wasn't what she had hoped for. She didn't know what to do.

The worry he had stored away in the back of his mind came rushing out like a tidal wave. He tried to defend himself. He tried to offer solutions. He said he had tried to be more present, but they wouldn't let him. The breakfast conversation didn't reach any resolution other than both of them agreeing that something had to change.

Later, on his own, he saw clearly that *he* was what had to change. Something in his life had to change. For some reason—he said he had no idea why—the idea popped into his head that he needed to get right with God. He needed God's help. He had never stopped going to Mass, and he considered himself a Catholic, but God was far away from his daily life. He needed to do something to get God involved.

And so he committed to a daily God time, to spending some time alone with God every single day. He created his own routine—a prayer journal, a list of people to pray for, a study Bible he would read from. It was nothing complicated —just twenty minutes alone with God at the start of every workday, in his office (he would close the door and instruct his executive assistant not to interrupt him until it was open again).

Almost as soon as he began to spend this short time in prayer every day, things started to change. Nothing on the outside changed—his wife still felt alone and overburdened; the kids still had issues; he still didn't know how to relate to them. But something inside him began to change. His reactions to those situations were different. He found interior light and the strength not to turn away from those challenges, but to wade right into them and humbly take the risks he needed to take in order to rebuild the most important relationships in his life.

At the time he told me this story, his family was strong and, as he put it, his original vision of what being a husband and father should be had been far surpassed by the reality. While things didn't change overnight, grace was now growing in his life, and it was showing its fruits.

A life of prayer is the soil in which the seed of grace can quicken, grow, and flourish, bearing the spiritual fruit that we all yearn for, because it's what we were made for. And every single one of us can develop a life of prayer. All we have to do is decide. Understanding what prayer really is can help make the decision a lot easier.

TWO
What Is Prayer?

If someone were to ask you, "Do you pray?" what would you say? What would come to mind about what it really means to pray?

As kids, most of us learned to say our prayers. Maybe this consisted of saying grace before meals and little else. Maybe it meant saying an Our Father in the morning and three Hail Marys at night before bed. Maybe it meant prayers before class at a Catholic school, or just knowing the responses at Sunday Mass. Maybe it even went so far as praying the Rosary together as a family sometimes.

SAYING PRAYERS?

Saying our prayers, however, is not the essence of a life of prayer. At least, not for those of us who have been given the privilege of knowing that Jesus Christ is the Savior, and that God is not a distant, heartless force, but a real person. In fact, the one true God, Creator of the universe and Redeemer of the human race, is actually a Trinity, an eternal being—all-knowing, all-loving, and all-powerful—who exists *in relationship*.

Jesus revealed this to us, and we acknowledge our faith in it every time we make the sign of the cross and pray, "In the name of the Father, and of the Son, and of the Holy Spirit." We pray in the *name* (singular) of the three Divine Persons (the Trinity).

Some non-Christians misunderstand this. They think that since we believe in the Blessed Trinity we actually believe in three Gods, that we're polytheists. When you try to explain to them that we really do believe in only one God, but a God who is three Persons, who is an eternal relationship of personal love (the love of the Father for the Son, the love of the Son for the Father, and the love between them, which is so full that it too is a Person, the Holy Spirit), they get confused. They don't understand how one God in three Persons can go together.

Actually, no one understands it—not completely, anyhow. Wouldn't it be strange if we, finite creatures with very limited intelligence, could fully understand the nature of God? If we could, would it really be worth believing in such a God? God is greater than we are. So we will never be able to exhaust our understanding of him. We will never completely figure him out, the way we can crack the code and solve a Rubik's Cube. There will always be more to discover and more to know when it comes to God.

But knowing that God is personal, that the divine mode of being is relationship, makes a huge difference for Christian prayer. And knowing that God has actually become man in Jesus Christ, in order to be close to us and to renew the life of grace by atoning for our sins, also makes a huge difference for Christian prayer. For us, prayer is never just a dry and sometimes fearful duty, or a complex and somewhat self-absorbed technique, as it is and has been for so many other religions throughout the expanse of human history. For us, the essence of prayer is *relationship*. It's not primarily about doing something, but about getting to know someone.

DON'T SNEEZE

For the vast majority of human history, from the appearance of the first fully human beings until early modern times, religion was as much a part of society as traffic, television screens, and twenty-four-hour news cycles are today. In fact, it was the central factor, the element that gave society its identity, direction, and values. And, of course, every religion involved prayer.

At its most basic level, prayer can be understood as communication between the human realm and the divine realm, between people and God. In pagan, polytheistic religions, prayer is almost always formalistic and ritualistic. In those religions, gods are simply immortal and powerful figures. They are not necessarily wise and loving, as we in post-Christian times are used to thinking of God. In fact, they are not even necessarily personal—some religions view their god as an impersonal, all-pervading force.

Because the pagan gods were considered powerful, people felt a need to stay in their good graces. This, they believed, would help assuage the negative impact of the many things outside human control—from the weather to the behavior of neighboring societies, and everything in between. But since these supposed divine forces weren't particularly interested in the human realm, prayers for assistance and protection weren't based on an intimate relationship. Rather, they were based on traditional rituals. If the rituals were followed correctly, so it was thought, the divine powers would be appeased, and the community could hope for stability and prosperity.

In that context, prayer was a formal duty. It was part of a ritual that could be used to express one's desires to the divine powers. But it was the proper performance of the ritual that mattered. For example, if a pagan priest was halfway through the ritual prayers and then happened to sneeze or cough or stutter, he would have to go back to the beginning and start all over again. Prayer, in essence, was about pushing the right buttons in order to keep the divine powers on your side.

This isn't to say that all rituals are empty and superficial. Rituals have always been part of human religious and social expression for a reason. They can help create an atmosphere set apart from normal, everyday activities. Ritual and tradition have a natural affinity for expressing and embodying what is sacred. And when it comes to worshipping the divine, whether a vague and mistaken notion of divinity as in pagan polytheism, or a true and fuller understanding of divinity through the revelation of Jesus Christ, a sense of the sacred is essential.

CONVERSATION WITH GOD

But rituals are not the stuff of life-changing prayer, from a Christian perspective. A believing, pious Muslim may faithfully, with proper intention, bow and kneel and recite sacred phrases while facing Mecca and adjusting the position of his hands and feet. In fact, doing just that five times a day is the essence of Islamic prayer. The mind and body and soul have thus been directed toward Allah in an expression of reverence beneficial to the believer, according to Islamic belief. This is the second of the Five Pillars (belief, prayer, almsgiving, fasting, and pilgrimage to Mecca) of Islam. It is a way of communicating with God. But from the Christian perspective, it is an extremely limited way.

Authentic religious piety may be present in that kind of prayer. And from their theological perspective, nothing else may be needed, because Islamic doctrine teaches that God is not a Trinity, and that God never became man in Jesus Christ in order to atone for our sins and enter into a real, interpersonal relationship with us.

But God *is* a Trinity, and through the Incarnation God *did* become man and has taken human nature to himself for all eternity. Therefore, when we communicate with God, we mustn't simply communicate through ritual and reverence. An additional dimension is essential. Christian prayer, at its very core, is the kind of communication that happens between two persons who know and love each other; it is a conversation that happens in relationship.

SERIOUSLY?

One of the most concise and moving expressions of this essence of Christian prayer is found in the *Catechism of the Catholic Church*, the entire fourth part of which is dedicated to explaining and describing the rich mystery of Christian praying. Here is how it defines Christian prayer:

> "Great is the mystery of the faith!" . . . This mystery, then, requires that the faithful believe in it, that they celebrate it, and that they live from it in a vital and personal relationship with the living and true God. *This relationship is prayer.* (*CCC*, 2558; emphasis added)

It's not just about saying prayers. It's not just about performing rituals. That's not what prayer life really is. Prayer life is an ongoing relationship, a personal, real, heart-to-heart friendship in which the two friends speak with each other about what is important to each of them.

This may seem like an exaggeration. After all, can't someone have a healthy relationship with God just by being a good person, following the commandments (more or less, anyway), and going to Mass on Sundays? Is it really necessary to have *conversations* with God? Is that even possible?

RELATIONSHIP AND CONVERSATION

Think about an important, meaningful relationship in your life. Now think about what would happen to that relationship if you never had any conversations with that person, if you never spent time together, just the two of you. Maybe you still see each other from a distance. Maybe you still go to the same events and hang out with the same groups of people. But you don't actually have any one-on-one exchanges anymore. How long would that relationship stay healthy? How long would it stay important and meaningful? How long would it continue to add value to your life? Not long.

That's the thing about God. He actually cares about you and me. He wants to be involved in our lives. He is interested in what's going on, in our struggles and hopes and projects and other relationships. And he has things he wants to give and say to us, words of comfort and wisdom and guidance and enlightenment.

Without giving up being God, our Creator and Redeemer, he always wants to be near us and walk with us, as our

Father and even as our friend. Jesus made this clear in so many ways, most especially when he told his followers at the Last Supper, "No longer do I call you servants, for the servant does not know what his master is doing; but I have called you friends, for all that I have heard from my Father I have made known to you" (John 15:15).

Only when God is present to us in that way—in a relationship in which we converse with our Lord and Savior as with a true friend—do our lives really get into gear and our hearts begin to find the meaning and joy they crave. And you simply can't have a meaningful friendship if you don't communicate and spend time together one-on-one.

Christian prayer is this personal, vital, ongoing relationship that each of us is invited to have with God.

A GIFT FOR YOU

Since prayer is a relationship with God, who by nature is beyond the reach of our limited powers of communication, it is also a true and, when you think about it, amazing gift.

This aspect of prayer often goes unrecognized. God didn't have to give us the possibility of lifting our hearts and minds to him, of knowing that he is always listening to us and always eager to converse with us. But he did. The revelation of Jesus Christ is a revelation of God's unflagging desire to be part of our lives, so that his grace can help us flourish in accordance with the true purpose and meaning of our deepest identity. To this end, he has promised to be present, to listen, to respond when we call on him, to accompany us no matter how far away from him we may wander.

The entire Bible is a history of God being faithful to this desire of his. The history of the Church, and in a special way the lives of our older brothers and sisters in the faith, the saints, show the same thing. God is always available to us. Prayer is always an option. From cornfields to concentration camps, from palaces to prisons, from grocery stores to gulags, God's loving interest in and dedication to us, his children whom he wants to become his friends, never wavers. To quote one of King David's most beloved psalms:

> O Lord, you have searched me and known me!
> You know when I sit down and when I rise up;
> you discern my thoughts from afar.
> You search out my path and my lying down,
> and are acquainted with all my ways.
> Even before a word is on my tongue,
> behold, O Lord, you know it altogether.
> You beset me behind and before,
> and lay your hand upon me.
> Such knowledge is too wonderful for me;
> it is high, I cannot attain it.
> (Psalm 139:1–6)

God truly is present to us and interested in our lives, and the gift of prayer is one of the most eloquent expressions of this. But it is a gift we must accept. God is always online, but we have to turn on the Wi-Fi to find him; we have to do our part to engage in a conversation with him. This is why one of the most famous descriptions of prayer in the history of the Church is the short and sweet definition from St. John

Damascene, a seventh-century Syrian monk: "Prayer is the raising of one's mind and heart to God or the requesting of good things from God."

THE ORIGINAL PRAYER BOOK

When we develop this relationship with God, this life of prayer, we create room in our lives for his grace to protect, purify, strengthen, and enlighten us. We have to believe this deeply and firmly; otherwise we will never be able to overcome the challenges that make developing this relationship so hard (we will talk more about these challenges later). One Old Testament image illustrates this reality with special eloquence: that of God as hideout. It comes from the Book of Psalms. The word *psalm* means "song." The Book of Psalms, which is right in the middle of the Bible, contains 150 songs, composed and gathered over the course of the Jewish people's long history of following God before the coming of Christ.

As part of the Bible, the psalms are inspired texts. This means, in part, that although real human authors wrote them (most, if not all, were written by King David, a great musician as well as a formidable warrior and leader), those authors were writing under the mysterious guidance of the Holy Spirit. The Holy Spirit wasn't dictating the Bible, as if the writers were in a trance and acting as automatons, but he was at work in the hearts and minds of the writers so that the many different books of the Bible are all inspired and sacred texts, and they all tell parts of the same story. Through what is written in the Bible, God has revealed himself in a special way. The words of the Bible are living words; they are God's words, and he continues to use them to communicate to us as a Church and as individuals. This is why the Bible is such an important text for Christian prayer and worship.

The psalms are sacred songs inspired by God. They express praise, petition, reflection, advice, exhortation, and even complaint. They are, in a sense, the prayer book of the Bible. Instead of simply describing events, as many of the biblical texts do, they are poems directed to God himself, composed under the direct inspiration of the Holy Spirit. In a sense, then, the psalms are a *school of prayer*. Since God inspired them, they show how he wants us to speak to him, and the descriptions of God that appear in them are descriptions of what he wants to be for us, if we let him.

In ancient Israel the Jewish people structured their communal prayer in the Temple around the psalms. The early Christians (many of whom were Jews who had come to believe that Jesus was the promised Messiah) followed suit, and eventually the Book of Psalms became the primary prayer book for the Church. They still are today. At every Mass, for example, we pray the "responsorial psalm" after the first reading from the Bible. These psalms embody the sentiments that the previous Scripture passage should stir up in a healthy Christian heart. They enable us to give words to the hopes, desires, and sufferings that we often feel but cannot easily express.

THE BEST HIDEOUT

That's a brief description of the Book of Psalms, in which God teaches us how to converse with him and reveals what he wants to be for us. It's necessary background for unpacking one of the most powerful images that appears in the psalms.

Often the psalmist addresses God in times of trouble, expressing faith-filled trust and confidence, which is as much a plea as an affirmation. In these passages, the inspired words refer to God as our rock, fortress, shield, and protector. In the middle of those litanies of trust, there sometimes appears another word, another image describing what God wants to be for us: our *hiding place*. For example: "The Lord is my rock-fastness, my stronghold, my rescuer; to God, *my hiding-place*, I flee for safety; he is my shield, my weapon of deliverance, my refuge" (Psalm 18:2, Knox translation; emphasis added).

The author of this psalm, King David, was not simply being poetic here. Although he was a gifted poet, he was also a warrior and a general. After he was anointed by the prophet Samuel to become the future king of Israel, he was violently persecuted by Saul, the current king, whose place he was ordained to take. Saul feared David and saw him as a usurper, and so he marshaled his troops to apprehend and kill him. Between his anointing and his accession to the throne, David spent more than a decade as a wanted man, an outlaw. He gathered his extended family around him, along with a few hundred other outcasts, and lived in hiding.

While avoiding King Saul's persecution and trying to convince him that he wasn't a usurper, David also continued to fight against Israel's enemies, the Philistines, with great success. But throughout this period, he and his band of followers basically lived in the wilderness of Palestine, in outlaw camps that could keep them safe from their persecutors.

And so, when David calls God his "rock-fastness . . . stronghold . . . rescuer . . . shield . . . refuge," he is not just speaking figuratively. He is expressing his confidence that

God's plan for his life is still unfolding, even though he is constantly facing mortal danger and dire difficulties. He hopes in God's promise and presence, in God's providence. Going to God in prayer is where he nourishes this hope and receives strength and light. God truly is, spiritually speaking, his "hiding-place"—or, to give it a more dynamic translation, his *hideout*.

In this period of David's life, he and his followers needed physical hideouts where they could be safe from their enemies, where they could heal the wounds they incurred in battle, repair their armor and weapons, refresh their strength, regroup, and make plans. At the same time, David personally needed a place of spiritual rest, recovery, and rejuvenation—a spiritual hideout. This is what he found in God through prayer. It is a striking and existential Old Testament image of what the *Catechism* means when it calls prayer a "vital and personal relationship with the living and true God."

THREE
Do We Really Need a Spiritual Hideout?

The key characteristic of a hideout is safety. It's a place where we can let down our guard, be ourselves, and recharge our mental, emotional, spiritual, and even physical energies. According to the inspired words of the Bible, this is what God wants to be for us; this is what he offers us through the mysterious and amazing gift of prayer.

But do we really need a hideout, a spiritual stronghold where we can take refuge and regroup? Yes, we do. Just like King David, all the great saints from the past, and Jesus himself, we need to develop a life of prayer through which God can become our hiding place, our spiritual hideout. This is true for at least four reasons: maintaining peace of mind and heart; developing quality relationships; finding shelter from storms and troubles; and experiencing lasting joy.

THE STRENGTH OF INTERIOR PEACE
First, we need to develop a life of prayer in order to maintain peace of mind and heart. Interior peace is necessary for lasting happiness, and for growing in all the worthwhile qualities

such as wisdom, compassion, courage, and patience. But it is constantly and violently threatened.

Our interior peace is under attack, in the first place, by sin—our sins and those of others. Sin is rebellion against God. It is leaving the path of authentic fulfillment, and it brings interior turbulence in its wake. Have you ever wondered why Jesus had to be scourged, beaten, crowned with thorns, and crucified in order to pay the price for the sins of the human family? Couldn't he have done it in a simpler and less painful way? One of the reasons for such a horrendous path to redemption was precisely to reveal to us the truth about sin. What Jesus' enemies did to his body during his passion and crucifixion is an image of what sin does to the human soul, to family relationships, to societies and cultures. And we are all affected by sin, by its violence and its destructive power, which ceaselessly threaten our interior peace.

But our peace of mind is also under attack from the instability and uncertainty of circumstances. So many external factors in life are outside our control: weather conditions and natural disasters, accidents and sickness, economic fluctuations, domestic and international political conflicts, and the list goes on. Because of recent advances in technology, we sometimes think we can insulate ourselves against these unpredictable and uncontrollable circumstances. We think that with the right bank balance, the right job, the right house, and the right friends, we can create a little heaven on earth where everything goes according to our wise and seemingly flawless plans.

Even though we know that's not true (because earth is just our pilgrim path to heaven), subconsciously we have a strong tendency to believe it. We have a deep-seated inclination to think we are capable of playing God in our lives and in the lives of our families and communities. Of course, we are not. And so unless this inclination is corralled and corrected, an omnipresent, subconscious layer of stress will constantly undermine our interior peace.

The simple fact is that we are sinners. We are not God. We cannot fix everything that is wrong all by ourselves, and we cannot perfectly manipulate life's circumstances. But we can't accept that truth fully unless we know that it's okay to have limits, that God can handle things even when we can't. Prayer nourishes us with that wisdom and viewpoint.

Without a life of prayer, without a spiritual hideout where we can go to be renewed and to nourish our faith and hope in God and the power of his loving providence, we simply cannot have true, lasting, fruitful interior peace. Here is how Pope Benedict XVI, one of the postmodern Church's greatest theologians, put it:

> It is easy to be entranced by the almost unlimited possibilities that science and technology place before us; it is easy to make the mistake of thinking we can obtain by our own efforts the fulfillment of our deepest needs. This is an illusion. Without God, who alone bestows upon us what we by ourselves cannot attain, our lives are ultimately empty. People need to be constantly reminded to cultivate a relationship with him who came that we might have life in abundance.[1]

---

[1] Pope Benedict XVI, "Celebration of Vespers and Meeting with the Bishops of the United States of America: Address of His Holiness Benedict XVI," Libreria Editrice Vaticana, April 16, 2008.

Those who pray never lose hope, even when they find themselves in a difficult and even humanly hopeless plight.[2]

GETTING UNSTUCK IN
OUR RELATIONSHIPS

In the end, relationships give real richness to our lives. Every human life is built around key relationships, starting with our family of origin and our oldest friendships, and moving on to include our own spouse and children, new friends and colleagues, teachers and mentors, and even employers and employees. Since we are created in God's image, and God is a Trinity—one divine nature, three divine Persons—our journey through time and space is a pilgrimage undertaken with others. The quality of our lives depends to a great extent on the quality of our relationships. To be known and loved by others, and to know and love them in return—this is the stuff of meaning and fulfillment. Even the most dramatic and impressive projects and achievements lose their luster when we have to enjoy them apart from deep, intimate, sincere, and truly satisfying relationships.

And yet, though most people would agree with this principle, they would also agree that relationships are one of the toughest parts of life. The more important the relationship, the harder it seems to be to keep it healthy, growing, fresh, and dynamic. Spouses often get to a point where they seem to be strangers to each other, even after years of living together and sharing so much. Parents and children are so easily estranged.

[2] Pope Benedict XVI, "General Audience," Libreria Editrice Vaticana, August 13, 2008.

Tensions at work lead to constant conflict, poisonous gossip, and destructive politics. Precisely because relationships are so central to the meaning of our lives as human beings, the corrosive effects of original sin show up there more intensely than anywhere else.

Developing a prayer life, learning to allow God to be our refuge, fortress, and hiding place, is the single greatest thing we can do to enhance our relationships, for the following reasons:

- Only God's grace can make us less defensive and fearful by revealing and healing the self-centeredness that subtly sabotages so many of our relationships.

- Only God's grace can teach us to truly understand other people from the inside out, to begin seeing them as God sees them, which allows us to accept them and value them without having to control and customize them.

- Only by experiencing God's loving presence and unfailing mercy in prayer do we find the strength to release the fears (of failure, of rejection, of humiliation) that undermine our ability to keep growing in intimacy and mutual trust.

- Only when we know that God has forgiven us, though we don't deserve his forgiveness, are we able to forgive others and make a fresh start as many times as needed.

To put it simply, by spending time with God we become more like God, and that means we become better spouses, parents, communicators, friends, professionals, sons and daughters—you name it. Prayer really is the proper soil for the growth of grace and all the fruits grace is meant to bring to our lives. To quote Pope Benedict XVI once again:

> Certainly the relationship with God is a profoundly personal matter, and the individual is a being in relationship with others. If the fundamental relationship with God is not living, is not lived, then no other relationship can find its right form. But this is also true for society, for humanity as such. Here, too, if God is missing, if God is discounted, if he is absent, then the compass is lacking which would show the way forward, the direction to follow in relationships as a whole.[3]

IN STORMS AND TROUBLES

King David needed hiding places for himself and his followers in the most literal sense possible: to avoid being attacked by enemy troops. In spiritually troubled times we too need a place of refuge. We may have the blessing of home, which has a roof and walls to protect us from meteorological storms, but life also sends emotional and spiritual storms. And the devil and his minions, our spiritual enemies, notch up the intensity of those storms whenever they can. We need shelter when that happens. We need a stronghold and a hiding place. We need a life of prayer.

[3] Pope Benedict XVI, "Celebration of Vespers with the Faithful of Aosta (Italy): Homily of His Holiness Benedict XVI," Libreria Editrice Vaticana, July 24, 2009.

Have you ever thought about how Jesus dealt with the evil attacks of his passion and crucifixion? He followed King David's plan and took refuge in his Father through prayer. That's what the famous scene from the Garden of Gethsemane is all about. He was on the eve of suffering massive betrayal, unjust condemnation, abandonment by his closest friends and followers, and unutterable physical torment. In addition to that, spiritual forces of darkness invaded his soul, causing so much anguish and stress that the capillaries under his skin burst from the pressure, causing him to sweat blood:

> And they went to a place which was called Gethsemane; and he said to his disciples, "Sit here, while I pray." And he took with him Peter and James and John, and began to be greatly distressed and troubled. And he said to them, "My soul is very sorrowful, even to death; remain here, and watch." And going a little farther, he fell on the ground and prayed that, if it were possible, the hour might pass from him. And he said, "Abba, Father, all things are possible to you; remove this cup from me; yet not what I will, but what you will." (Mark 14:32–36)

> And being in an agony he prayed more earnestly; and his sweat became like great drops of blood falling down upon the ground. (Luke 22:44)

Jesus was fully human, but he was also fully divine: "God from God, light from light, true God from true God," as we pray every week in the Creed. And even as a man, he had none of the effects of original sin that we suffer from, which create in us so much interior division and disproportionate emotional distress. And yet, in spite of his unique condition and gifts, Jesus Christ experienced the same kind of agony and crisis that each one of us has to go through at some point in our earthly pilgrimage. And how did he deal with it? He prayed. He went off to be alone with his Father, and he prayed. That's where he found the strength to fulfill his mission, to endure his sufferings, to be faithful in the face of so much betrayal and opposition.

If Jesus Christ needed prayer in order to carry his cross, how much more will we need a life of prayer to be able to carry ours!

A WOMAN IN DENVER

I will never forget an encounter I had with a woman in the Denver airport. I had found a quiet corner near a gate that wasn't being used, because I wanted to pray. I was walking back and forth, away from the other travelers, holding my rosary behind my back and praying silently, looking down at the ground. Suddenly, as I made my third or fourth turn, a woman was standing right in front of me. I couldn't continue my meditative walk, so I looked up. She was a tall woman in her forties, with spiked hair, dressed in black. She was looking at me intensely, her eyes and face wrenched with anguish and deep distress. I smiled and said hello, a little shocked. And she answered, in a northern European accent: "Father, will you please pray with me?"

The question threw me for a loop. People often ask me to pray *for* them when they notice my Roman collar and realize I am a priest. But up until that point, no one had ever asked me to pray *with* them. Seeing the absolute sincerity, almost desperation, of her request, I said, "Of course!" We both bowed our heads, standing close together, and I began to pray in my own words, asking God to touch our hearts and send us the grace we needed.

After about a minute, it dawned on me that this woman probably had something specific weighing on her heart, something concrete that we should pray about. So I interrupted my prayer, looked at her and asked, "Is there anything specific you would like to pray for?" When she looked up, tears were streaming down her face. Between her sobs, she answered, "My mother . . . my mother just died." So much sorrow filled those words!

It wasn't the moment to ask for more details, and she clearly wasn't able to have a conversation about it right then, but I could imagine the interior struggle, the spiritual storm she was going through. Either she and her mother had been very close and the circumstances of her death were tearing this woman apart, or perhaps they had been estranged and opportunities for reconciliation had come and gone, and now were no more. In any case, feeling her pain, I bowed my head and we both prayed from the depths of our hearts for her mother and for her, and for God's grace to bring light, strength, and peace out of the tragic loss.

When I sensed a feeling of acceptance and release of tension, we prayed the Our Father together and made the Sign of the Cross. Then I looked up again, hoping to engage her in some conversation and offer some words of comfort. But she simply looked at me, still crying, but now with profound relief and hope in her eyes. Then she walked away, saying, "Thank you, Father, thank you."

Here was a woman with a deep spiritual sensitivity, but she had no hiding place, no refuge—she wasn't a pray-er. A spiritual storm swept in and hit her hard, and she knew she couldn't weather it alone. But, for whatever reason, her own prayer life was either dormant or too underdeveloped to allow her to find a stronghold in the Lord. God in his providence intervened and helped her.

Right now, by inviting you to jump-start your prayer life, he is doing the same for you. He wants you to be prepared for the crosses that this fallen world will surely lay upon your soul. He wants to be your refuge and your hiding place.

THE KEY TO LASTING JOY

Joy is the satisfaction that comes from possessing something good and knowing that we do. Material and earthly joys are by nature passing. I can *enjoy* a brownie as long as it lasts, and I can experience the delicious taste. But by its very nature as a material thing, it doesn't last very long.

Christian joy, the fruit of the Holy Spirit, is different. It can last, because it is a spiritual joy based on the possession of spiritual truth that fills our hearts more than any pastry ever could. Through our faith, we know that we are infinitely loved by God, that he created us with a purpose, that he has forgiven and will continue to forgive all our sins, and that Jesus has gone before us into heaven to prepare a place for us there, a place of everlasting fulfillment and bliss. Through our faith we know that we are not a mistake or a random product of evolution; we are thoroughly known, valued, loved, and accepted by God himself. In turn, he calls us to know him, to love him, and even to contribute to the building up of his everlasting kingdom.

These are truths that never change. When they resonate with our heart, they bring us deep joy that can outlast life's changing circumstances and painful troubles. Knowing these truths satisfies the deepest longings of our hearts: the longing for meaning and purpose, as well as to be loved and to be able to love in a total, definitive way. And it is our life of prayer that allows our knowledge of these truths to penetrate our soul more and more completely. In fact, only a life of prayer, in which we learn how to turn our attention to the God who is always paying loving attention to us, can transform these truths from abstract catechetical affirmations into existential fountains of spiritual energy and life-giving light. If we lack a life of prayer, we lose contact with these truths, and their power to enrich and strengthen us diminishes until it disappears.

MEMORY LAPSE

In the Old Testament, one of God's big complaints against his chosen people, Israel, has to do with their short memory. Many, many times he intervened dramatically in their history to show them how valued and protected they were. Liberation from Egypt, manna in the desert, entering the Promised Land . . . over and over again, God showed his faithfulness, mercy, love, and power, and proved that his people had nothing to fear. And yet, over and over again, his people would forget. This forgetfulness led them to doubt his presence and his care, which led them to search for security and meaning along the self-destructive paths of idolatry and sin. Here is a typical example of God's complaint against Israel for their short memory: "They did not keep God's covenant, but refused to walk according to his law. *They forgot what he had done*, and the miracles that he had shown them" (Psalm 78:10–11; emphasis added).

In past generations, when our culture was still Christian, still built around the rhythms of the liturgical year and the values of the gospel, society itself provided a continual flow of reminders about how much God is committed to us, how much our life means in his eyes, how unconditionally, passionately, and personally we are loved by the Lord. But now our secularized culture has succeeded in extracting the message of Jesus from public discourse and everyday life. Instead, we are bombarded by information about new products, new exercise programs, new entertainment, alarming and sensational tragedies, and political squabbles.

In order to live in tune with the deeper truths, the truths that fill our inner life with joy no matter what's happening on the outside, we must learn to remember the Word of God and all he has revealed to us. We must learn to make the Lord our hiding place, and let his grace be the motor of our lives. Here the Blessed Virgin Mary sets an inspiring example. God worked wonders in her life, and she didn't forget about them: "But Mary kept all these things, pondering on them in her heart" (Luke 2:19).

This lasting joy that comes from maintaining in our minds and hearts a conscious awareness of these deeper truths, the ones that satisfy our deepest longings, is not an illusion. It is real. When we set out on the path to spiritual maturity, this joy begins to grow and spread in our lives. We have to persevere in our life of prayer in order to keep maturing, but we can taste it and hope for more of it even at the beginning of the journey, and that in itself helps us become more joyful human beings.

A GUY IN ROME

Toward the end of his life, St. John Paul II was sick and weak. He continued to follow his backbreaking papal schedule, but various ailments were limiting his mobility, as well as his capacity to speak. He refused to withdraw from public life, even when his illnesses and the medications he was required to take began to have a visible effect on his body, making him truly look like a sick old man. But he felt that part of his Christian witness consisted of showing that even the pope lived in solidarity with every form of human suffering. And so he kept up his public appearances.

Those appearances included what are called *ad limina* visits from all the bishops of the world. Every five years, each Catholic bishop comes to Rome with the other bishops from his area, and they meet with the pope. They receive guidance, instruction, and encouragement, and they inform the pope and the Vatican cardinals about what's happening in their dioceses.

On one occasion, a young American bishop was making his first *ad limina* visit to Rome. His whole priesthood had been lived under the inspiration of St. John Paul II, whose papacy is the second longest in history, and he was eager and excited to finally have a chance to meet the Holy Father in person. At this point, John Paul II was well advanced in his years, his illnesses, and his suffering. Everyone could tell that he didn't have much time left on this earth.

When the young bishop had his chance to speak to the Holy Father, he finished their exchange by expressing his heartfelt gratitude for all the pope had done and been for him and for so many other priests he knew. Then at the end of their encounter, before he had to return to the United States, he said to the Holy Father, "Your holiness, it has been such a privilege and a joy to meet with you. My only regret is that I won't be able to see you again five years from now." John Paul II, visibly in pain and weakened by his medications, looked at the young bishop with a mischievous twinkle in his eye and joked, "Oh, really? I didn't know you were ill."

Christian joy is an interior well of vitality and contagious optimism based on eternal truths. It is accessible only inside the spiritual hideout that is our life of prayer. It is where St. John Paul II, like so many other saints who have found and fulfilled their life's mission, drew all his spiritual refreshment.

When we develop a life of prayer, we can learn to say with the prophet Habakkuk:

> Though the fig tree do not blossom,
> nor fruit be on the vines,
> the produce of the olive fail
> and the fields yield no food,
> the flock be cut off from the fold
> and there be no herd in the stalls,
> yet I will rejoice in the Lord
> I will joy in the God of my salvation.
> (Habakkuk 3:17–18)

The deeper our connection to God, the greater our capacity for joy, regardless of the challenges and losses that affect us. This too is why God wants to be our hideout and our refuge by leading us into a vital and personal relationship with him through prayer.

FOUR
Getting Practical: How Do We Pray?

The essence of prayer is the ongoing relationship each one of us is meant to have with God, and the heart-to-heart communication that nourishes such a relationship. But what exactly does this look like in practice? How does it happen? What is our role and what is God's role? Now we're ready to tackle questions like those.

THE 2-3 COMBINATION

The essence of prayer is a *relationship*, but the practice of prayer is an *activity*. The ultimate goal of our prayer life is to reach spiritual maturity, to get to the point where we never lose awareness of God's presence, where we live in a continual interior dialogue with him. As we move in that direction, we engage in two *kinds* of prayer activities: personal and communal. We also engage in three *forms* of prayer activities: vocal, mental, and liturgical.

Failing to understand this 2–3 combination (the two kinds and three forms of prayer) is one of the most common obstacles to growing in prayer. When we mix all these kinds and forms of prayer together, we are also mixing together various expectations of what prayer should feel like. Without realizing it, we can get tangled up, connecting a legitimate expectation to a form of prayer that can never really fulfill that expectation. Discouragement, confusion, or frustration (or all three) is the result. So let's take some time to unpack these core ideas.

PERSONAL PRAYER

Each one of us has a personal and unique relationship with God. For this relationship to grow and flourish, we have to spend quality time alone with him, just the two of us. Here is how Jesus explained it: "But when you pray, go into your room and shut the door and pray to your Father who is in secret; and your Father who sees in secret will reward you" (Matthew 6:6).

Throughout the history of the Church, saints and spiritual writers have developed an increasing awareness of the importance of personal prayer—of, as the fifteenth-century nun, foundress, and doctor of the Church St. Teresa of Ávila put it, "spending time alone with the One I know loves me." This is personal prayer, one-on-one time with the Lord, who deserves our praise and whose grace we need.

In personal prayer we go at our own pace. We discover what helps us as individuals to hear God's voice in our hearts and to respond generously. We learn to engage in an intimate dialogue with the Lord that has unique characteristics. No one else relates to God in exactly the same way you do, so no one else's personal prayer will be exactly the same as yours.

Certain principles are universally present in personal prayer, which we will explore in the following sections, but even those universal principles take unique shape in each person's case. It's like walking and the laws of physics. The laws of physics—gravity, friction, momentum, acceleration, and muscle flexing and contracture—are the same for all of us. And yet everyone's walk is a little bit different. You can identify an individual person from a distance simply by the way he or she walks. In a similar way, if we give space to prayer in our lives and follow the basic principles, each one of us gradually develops a unique style and experience of personal prayer.

COMMUNAL PRAYER

Unlike some non-Christian spiritualties and religions, the Christian vision of spiritual maturity is not individualistic. The unique, personal relationship that each of us has with God is essential and irreplaceable, but it exists in the context of a wider network of relationships. Each one of us, through baptism, becomes a child of God. That means we are members of God's family. We don't fly solo in the Christian adventure; we have brothers and sisters, and our personal story forms part of a much bigger story of salvation.

St. Paul, in his New Testament letters, goes even one step further. Through the divine life, the grace, present in the soul of everyone who is baptized, he explains, we all become members of the mystical body of Christ:

> For just as the body is one and has many members, and all the members of the body, though many, are one body, so it is with Christ. For by one Spirit we were all baptized into one body—Jews or Greeks, slaves or

free—and all were made to drink of one Spirit.
(1 Corinthians 12:12–13)

For as in one body we have many members, and all
the members do not have the same function, so we,
though many, are one body in Christ, and individually
members one of another. (Romans 12:4–5)

In other words, Christians are never Lone Rangers. We are
part of a spiritual family, the Church, to which each one of
us contributes in accordance with the spiritual gifts we have
received from God, and through which each of us is enriched
by the spiritual gifts of all the others.

Because of this, our relationship with God is not just
personal; it is also communal, familial, ecclesial. So our
prayer life—the activities through which we communicate
with God to foster his grace in our lives—also needs to have
a communal, familial, and ecclesial dimension. In addition
to the one-on-one time with God that we all find in personal prayer, then, we need to spend time with God in the
company of our brothers and sisters in the faith. The most
obvious way we do this is through Sunday Mass. But it also
has other manifestations: spouses praying together for their
children; family Rosaries; parish holy hours and penance
services; grace before meals; benedictions before and after
important events; spontaneous prayers at the beginning or
end of a faith-sharing group's gathering.

When we pray together, we imagine God, who is a
Trinity, in a special way. Communal prayer is not always as
comfortable as personal prayer, because it doesn't necessarily

follow one's preferred pace or expressions, but it too is an essential element in the development of an authentic life of prayer. Jesus himself made this clear, explaining the mystical power behind communal prayer:

> "Again I say to you, if two of you agree on earth about anything they ask, it will be done for them by my Father in heaven. For where two or three are gathered in my name, there am I in the midst of them."
> (Matthew 18:19–20)

Praying together is important. Communal prayer and personal prayer are like the two legs we use to walk the journey of faith. We need them both.

FORM 1: VOCAL PRAYER

We have looked briefly at the two basic kinds of prayer, personal and communal. Now we need to get into the three different forms of prayer: vocal, mental, and liturgical. It may sound a little complicated, but it's really not that bad. And unless we make these distinctions, it will be impossible to adjust our expectations to avoid unnecessary frustration and stultification.

Vocal, *mental*, and *liturgical* are technical terms. They have emerged from centuries of experience and theological reflection. Different authors and speakers sometimes use them in slightly different or overlapping ways, but getting clear about their core meaning will give you a huge advantage as you renew your prayer life.

Vocal prayer is simply praying with someone else's words, whether personally or communally, out loud or silently. When we learned to "say our prayers," we learned vocal prayer. The Our Father, the Hail Mary, the Prayer of St. Francis—these are vocal prayers. When we pray them, we take the words that someone else has come up with and we make them our own, using them to lift our hearts and minds to God. Vocal prayer is that simple.

The key in vocal prayer is to mean what we say when we say it. The words, whether taken from the Bible or the liturgy, or composed by saints or other spiritual writers, are full of meaning. They express certain aspects of the truth about God, the world, and us. When we mean what we say when we pray them, the power of those truths is released in our minds and hearts. Using these prayers is like exercising the muscles of our souls, the deep convictions that help us think, speak, and act like true Christians. And the truths contained in these prayers become a way for our hearts to connect with God's heart: We use them to express what's in our souls, and he in turn, through the revealed truths these words contain, comforts and enlightens us.

A GUY IN SOLITARY CONFINEMENT

Cardinal Francis Xavier Nguyen Van Thuan was appointed Archbishop of Saigon, Vietnam, on April 24, 1975, during the Vietnam War. Six days later Saigon fell to the Communist North Vietnamese Army. Since communism is an atheist ideology and totalitarian system, the conquerors quickly went to work trying to absorb or dismantle the Catholic Church there. They targeted the archbishop as part of their strategy. First, they tried to convince him to support their regime. But he refused, because getting behind the Communist Party would require surrendering the Church to their control and validating their atheistic philosophy.

So the Communist authorities changed tactics. They tried to force him to cave in to their demands. They detained him. They put him under house arrest. They sent him to reeducation camps. All together, they spent thirteen years trying to break down his resolve. For nine of those years, the future cardinal was subject to solitary confinement. It didn't work. In the end, after immense suffering and many amazing, even miraculous events and courageous deeds, Archbishop Van Thuan was released, on the condition that he leave the country and never come back. He spent the rest of his life in exile in Rome, where he was made cardinal and continued to inspire Catholics all over the world with his wisdom, faith, and testimony. He died in 2002.

During his solitary confinement, at one point Archbishop Van Thuan was confined in a cell too narrow for him to lie down full length and too short for him to stand up completely. It was stiflingly hot, and the only fresh air he could find emerged from a drain in the floor. To breathe easily, he had to keep his face close to the drain, a gathering place for centipedes and roaches and other vermin. He was maltreated and malnourished, unsure whether he would live or die, or simply go insane from the suffering.

In those conditions, prayer was extremely difficult. But it turned out to be what enabled him to keep his faith, his determination, his wits, and even his sense of humor. And in the toughest times, when he could barely think straight, it was *vocal* prayer that became his refuge and his hiding place.

All he could do in his exhaustion and pain was recite short vocal prayers, words from the Bible, or phrases from the liturgy. These short prayers became a spiritual life raft. The power of their truth kept his spirit strong even as his body wasted away. Here is how he explained it in his testimonial book, *Five Loaves & Two Fish*: "I who am weak and mediocre, I love these short prayers.... The more I repeat them, the more I am penetrated by them. I am close to You, Lord."[4]

He would feed his soul on these inspired words, on prayers that someone else had written. He would mull them over, let them sink in, let their truth penetrate him, use them to make sense out of his suffering, let God speak to him through them, and let his heart respond to God through them. That's what vocal prayer is all about.

SAYING YOUR FAVORITE PRAYERS

We should all have some favorite vocal prayers that we can recite in good times and bad, prayers we can use to turn our attention to God at the beginning of the day, at the end of the day, and whenever we feel the turbulent pressures of this fallen world. Vocal prayers are often set to music as hymns or other songs. Singing or listening to them can be a powerful way to converse with God.

Vocal prayer is especially useful when we are really busy, or sick, or in the midst of some trial, like Cardinal Van Thuan was. In those situations, the precise and clear meaning of those prayers gives us comfort, wisdom, and perspective, even as it helps us express to God the desires, hopes, and sorrows that sometimes we ourselves cannot find the right words to express.

[4] Francis Xavier Nguyen Van Thuan, *Five Loaves & Two Fish* (New York: Pauline Books and Media, 2003).

Take, for example, the first verse of Blessed John Henry Newman's famous prayer poem, "Lead, Kindly Light."[5] The first line includes the title: "Lead, kindly light, amid the encircling gloom, lead Thou me on." Already in those few words we find a wealth of truth that can nourish our souls. By addressing God as a "kindly light," we are exercising our faith in his existence, in his goodness, and in his gentle but committed interest in our lives. By asking him to lead us on "amid the encircling gloom," we are exercising our confidence, our trust, and our hope in him. At the same time, we are giving voice to the reality of our own weakness, sinfulness, confusion, and sorrow. Already, in the first line of this poem, we are connecting with the deeper truths, truths we can build our lives around.

The prayer continues, "The night is dark, and I am far from home." Here again we exercise our faith, this time affirming, and thereby strengthening, our belief in heaven, our true home. We acknowledge that our earthly lives are a journey, and that they have a destination, a purpose.

Then Blessed Newman writes, "Keep Thou my feet, I do not ask to see the distant scene, one step enough for me." Here the prayer goes back to the theme of humility and trust. By requesting God's help simply to take the next step in his life journey, "one step enough for me," he resists the perennial temptation to try to control everything, the temptation of pride and arrogance: "I do not ask to see the distant scene."

This is the inner dynamic of vocal prayer. The meaning of the words that make up these prayers, whether they are taken

[5] From John Henry Newman's poem, "The Pillar of the Cloud," written in 1833.

directly from the Bible or simply composed in harmony with the message of Christ, become a place of encounter between the soul and God. Through these words and their Christian meanings, we lift our minds and hearts to him, and he touches us with his grace. We open ourselves to receive light and strength, and he reaches down to give them to us.

And in times of exceptionally intense joy or anguish, the words of familiar vocal prayers simply become a vehicle to express the inexpressible—we offer up an Our Father or a Hail Mary, and we infuse their familiar words with the unutterable yearnings of our hearts.

FORM 2: MENTAL PRAYER

The danger with vocal prayer is succumbing to routine. The words can become so familiar that it's hard for us to keep meaning what we say when we pray them. As a result, if vocal prayer is the only form of prayer we ever learn, we can easily get bored with it. In that case, prayer gradually comes to feel irrelevant and useless. We sense that we have outgrown prayer because "saying our prayers" has become an empty shell.

For Christians, vocal prayer was never meant to be the only form of prayer. We are called not only to use ready-made prayers, biblically inspired or otherwise, but also to speak to God in our own words, to have a real conversation with him. This personal conversation with the Lord, in which we listen to him and respond in our own words, is the essence of mental prayer.

It is called "mental" because it takes place deep within our minds and hearts. It is an interior encounter with God, a being in his presence—and God dwells within: "The kingdom of God is in the midst of you" (Luke 17:21).

Mental prayer has two essential elements: listening and responding. In mental prayer, we take time to quiet our minds and turn our attention to what God is saying to us. We consider it, mull it over, savor it. And then we respond to it in our own words. Maybe we respond by thanking God, or by praising him. We may respond by asking him for something we need, or expressing our sorrow and repentance for sins.[6] The response flows from whatever we hear God speak to our hearts.

HEARING GOD'S VOICE

How do we listen to God? He speaks in many ways. The most direct way is through his written Word, the Bible. We listen to him there by reading a passage from the Bible slowly and pensively, pausing to consider what it means *for me* in the here and now of my life and what God wants to say *to me* through it.

We can also listen through reflective reading of good spiritual books that comment on the Bible or on the truths of our faith—even the *Catechism* can be used in mental prayer. God also speaks through beauty—art, music, and nature. These too can be sources that we delve into, that we listen to, when we take time for mental prayer.

And, of course, God speaks through the events of our lives and the lives of those around us. His providence is real, so we can also discover him speaking to us through the unfolding of our personal history and the history of salvation as a whole.

---

[6] The acronym PASTA encapsulates the different types of response we can address to the Lord: Praise, Adoration, Sorrow, Thanksgiving, Asking.

Taking time for this personal conversation with God is absolutely essential for spiritual growth. Each of us is unique, and so each of us has—and is meant to have—a unique relationship with God, a real friendship. That can only develop if we spend time in this kind of personal exchange. Mental prayer, by its very nature, is more personalized than vocal prayer. It gives God space to enlighten and guide us in a customized way. Unless mental prayer becomes a staple of our spiritual lives, God's grace will simply not have sufficient room to make us truly flourish.

CHRISTIAN MEDITATION

Through the centuries, many methods have arisen that can help give structure to mental prayer. And structure is useful, especially in the first stages of spiritual growth. These methods are usually referred to as ways of doing Christian meditation. In this context, the word *meditation* is simply a synonym for "mental prayer." It means focused and prayerful reflection that becomes a conversation with God.

Here is a simple but powerful structure (gleaned from a study of many different traditions) for Christian meditation. It has four steps: concentrate, consider, converse, commit. Christian meditation is not some arcane spiritualist technique reserved for monks and hermits. Everyone should do it—including you. Here's how:

Concentrate

The first step is to quiet our busy minds and focus our attention on God. You wouldn't try to have a meaningful conversation with your buddy while you were both madly multitasking and trying to get your own work done, and the same goes for our friendship with God. We have to turn off the smartphone, find a quiet place and a recollected posture, and let our minds settle. If we don't, there is no way we will be able to hear what God wants to tell us.

To help with this step, it's useful to have a regular time and place for personal prayer. This creates a rhythm and fosters habits conducive to recollection. Some people like chapels or churches. Others like their study or a little prayer corner somewhere in their house, set up with a candle and a holy image. There are some who find a small fishing boat on a scenic river to be a perfect place, especially in light of the first apostles being fishermen. Some like to have their prayer time in the morning (most spiritual writers agree that this is ideal—it starts the day out right, keeping first things first), but others can make time only in the evening. Some go to a nearby parish during their lunch break. It's also useful to decide ahead of time how long you will spend in prayer. If you have decided to give fifteen minutes to the Lord every morning, that clarity will help you focus as your prayer time gets started.

Another practical aid for this step is to plan ahead about what you will be using to feed your conversation with God— your Bible, a spiritual book, a book of meditations, the readings from Mass, a prayer journal in which you can write out your thoughts and sentiments to help keep them focused as you converse with the Lord.

Having your time, place, and supplies ready ahead of time makes it easy to enter into God's presence and start your meditation. A good way to begin a meditation is by using a favorite vocal prayer, or simply by making the traditional acts of faith, hope, and love. That just means telling God that you truly do believe in him, and in all he has revealed; that you really are hoping in his grace and his goodness to lead you to a fulfilling life here and now on earth and forever in heaven; that you love him; that you want to follow Jesus and obey his commandments and do your part to help build up his kingdom. When you finish your initial vocal prayer or acts of faith, hope, and love, you can ask the Lord to bless this time; ask for the grace you need, for whatever is on your heart.

Once you are calmed down and focused on the Lord, you are ready to listen. That's the next step.

Consider
Here is where you stop talking and start listening. You open the book you are using to help your meditation, or you gaze at the beautiful sunrise or holy image, or you call to mind something you experienced yesterday that resonated deeply with you. You actively turn your mind to consider whatever it is you have decided to meditate on. In this step, you are searching for what God wants to say to you. And you will recognize it when something strikes a chord in your heart, giving you light or making you experience a good, holy desire. As soon as it does, pause, and savor that idea or that good desire. Allow it to fill your soul and nourish your spirit. The resonance that you experience as you consider that saving truth, whatever form it takes, is how God is speaking to you. That's what he wants you to listen to. When that chord strikes in your heart and you allow it to expand and reverberate, you are ready for the third step.

Converse

Here is where you respond to what God has spoken to your soul. And your response will depend on what type of insight you receive.

For example, you may be meditating on a crucifix, or on the description of the crucifixion in St. Matthew's Gospel. And you may find yourself struck by the fact that Jesus really didn't deserve to suffer any of this, but he voluntarily gave himself up in order to pay the price for our sins. Your heart may be moved by a sense of sorrow for the times when you have ignored God's commandments or disobeyed his voice in your heart—those sins contributed to Christ's crucifixion. And so your response may be one of simply telling God that you are sorry for those sins, that you don't want to sin anymore. You may want to ask him to give you the strength to avoid sin in the future, and to forgive your past sins.

On the other hand, you may be meditating on the same scene from Christ's life, but find yourself struck by something else entirely. For instance, the form of the cross may inspire you: the vertical beam connecting heaven and earth, and the horizontal beam embracing the whole world. Jesus is the mediator between God and the human family; he has brought us together through his self-sacrifice on the cross, and he continues to bring us together at every Mass, where the priest lifts the host and the chalice up toward heaven and then distributes the Eucharist to all the faithful who are gathered there. This thought may resonate, and move you to respond with words or sentiments of deep wonder, praise, and gratitude. Or it may fill you with a desire to receive Holy Communion more worthily.

In this step of the meditation, you put into your own words a response to what you have heard God speak to your soul. Sometimes, however, you may not be able to find the words, and the wordless yearning or wonder of your heart will be the entirety of your response.

Commit

When you have said what you have to say, or when the sense of resonance subsides, you can go back to whatever you are meditating on and continue to consider it (for example, read slowly the next paragraph or passage), until something else strikes your heart. Then stay with that, and respond to it, without rushing. The interaction between step 2 (consider) and step 3 (converse) can happen multiple times in a single meditation.

Sooner or later, however, the time you have set aside for prayer will come to an end. At this point, it's important to finish well. An overly abrupt conclusion to your prayer is like a rude parting between friends. You need to wrap things up naturally and intelligently. You can do this by writing down the most striking insights or desires that came up in your prayer, or writing a little note to the Lord, for example. This renews your general commitment to be his faithful follower throughout the coming day.

Another way to conclude your meditation is to make a specific resolution or commitment as a result of what you have meditated on. This could be something as simple as "I am going to call my brother and see how he is doing," or "I am going to sign up for that weekend retreat that I keep putting off," or "Today I will make a special effort, with your help, Jesus, not to lose my patience at the office," or "Today

I will keep in mind the line from Psalm 23: 'The Lord is my shepherd, I shall not want,' especially when I am feeling stressed or fearful."

We are not angels. We are still in the midst of life's journey, engaged in the spiritual battle of human history; we need to make decisions about how we are going to live out our Christian discipleship. When those decisions flow from our prayer, we know they will be fruitful.

Once you have renewed your commitment to Christ and his kingdom by making some kind of decision or resolution, you can finish with a favorite vocal prayer (an Our Father and a Hail Mary, for example, or any other you may like), make the Sign of the Cross, and move on with the rest of your day.

CHRISTIAN CONTEMPLATION

As the adventure of your prayer life unfolds, you will find that sometimes when you are meditating, God's presence seems to take over. You lose yourself in an awareness of his goodness and his love. In these moments, the exchange that happens between your soul and God goes beyond words. It's almost like an embrace, or a simple spiritual contentment at being with the Lord.

When this happens, you do not need to force yourself to consider and converse. Rather, just accept the gift that God is giving you. When he makes his presence felt in this way—and it really does come from him, freely and mysteriously; nothing we can do can force this to happen—his grace enriches and nourishes us without the mediation of our own searching, pondering, or thinking. This is, in general, what

Christian tradition calls "contemplation" or "contemplative prayer."

Volumes have been written on these terms, and entire schools of spirituality have developed in order to understand more fully what is really happening when God takes over in our prayer. We don't need to go into detail about this right now. It's enough to know that sometimes our mental prayer (yes, contemplation, like meditation, is under the umbrella of mental prayer) goes through moments or seasons of great simplicity, in which we don't have to work very hard to find God's presence and hear what he is saying to us. When those seasons come, we can embrace and enjoy them. When we don't really understand them, we can always find someone with a bit more experience to help us figure it out.

CHRISTIAN YOGA?

Mental prayer, meditation, contemplation—these are concepts sometimes associated with non-Christian spiritual traditions. You may have heard of Transcendental Meditation (linked to Buddhism), for instance, or you may be familiar with yoga (which has its roots in the Hindu religion) and the meditative techniques that often go along with it. Should this worry us? Or are all religions basically the same anyway?

The answer to both questions is no: No, this should not worry us; and no, all religions are not basically the same.

The key thing to remember here is that Christian prayer is essentially the unfolding of our relationship with God. It is an encounter between two real people: you and God. In prayer, we seek to know God better, to thank and praise him, and to let him guide and strengthen us. At the same time, he truly is listening to us, and he has things he wants to say to us, gifts he wants to give us. Christian prayer, whether mental (meditative or contemplative), vocal, or liturgical, is always a face-to-face reality: We seek God's face, and he lovingly gazes at ours.

For a Christian, then, meditation is never a technique to achieve inner tranquility. It is never merely a tool used in pursuit of self-absorption, or a path of self-discipline designed to force or to fabricate a mystical experience. Non-Christian meditation is often about those things. It is a self-centered activity, not a God-directed conversation.

But watch out, because once God allows you to experience the sweetness of his presence in prayer, you will like it. And you may start wanting to experience that sweetness all the time. So you may start going to prayer and following your method of meditation just to reproduce that sweetness, which is a bad idea. That confuses the gift (the occasional sweetness or consolation that God sends us when we need it) with the giver of the gift (God himself). The path to spiritual maturity is to seek God and his will for our lives, not to lust after intense feelings.

Remember, we pray in order to grow in our relationship with God. If he wants to give us intense and delightful experiences, great. But if he doesn't, if instead he wants us to keep seeking him and exercising our faith even when we don't feel his presence at all, when we just feel dryness and experience darkness, that's great too! God knows what we need. We pray because he deserves our praise and we need his grace. We pray because we are involved in a relationship, a friendship with the Lord, not because we want to get a spiritual high. In other words, prayer isn't like yoga, just clearing our minds and making our muscles relax. It goes beyond body and brain to satisfy heart and soul.

FORM 3: LITURGICAL PRAYER

Vocal prayer can be done personally or communally. You may have guessed already that mental prayer can only be done personally—it is that intimate. At times we may share with others what has happened in our mental prayer or reflect together on the Sacred Scriptures, and we may pray spontaneously out loud in our own words when we are gathered with others. But the intimate exchange, the highly personal listening and responding that characterizes mental prayer, is essentially an individual encounter with God. The third form of prayer, liturgical prayer, is the contrary. Although it can be engaged in with others or individually, it is always communal.

The etymological roots of the word *liturgy* mean "the work of the people." By its nature, liturgical prayer is the prayer of the whole Church, of the family of God. For this reason, it is governed by officially recognized rubrics and norms, which give us, for example, the liturgical year with all its holidays—a word that comes to us as a derivative of "holy days." They also give us the formulas and rituals that we use at Mass and for all the other sacraments—marriage, baptism, confirmation, anointing of the sick, and holy orders. They give us daily prayers too, called the Liturgy of the Hours, which weave together psalms, traditional prayers and hymns, and other passages from the Bible in a beautiful, rhythmic, and symbolic ensemble of vocal prayer that all members of the clergy and all members of religious orders are required to pray on a regular basis by Church law (known as "canon law"). The Liturgy of the Hours includes vespers (evening prayer) and lauds (morning prayer), along with three other daily offices. Although laypeople are not required to participate in the Liturgy of the Hours, the Church cordially invites them to do so.

As you can see, liturgical prayer is ample and rich. It is always going on. By means of it, the Church throughout the world, as Christ's mystical body and bride, continues to offer praise and worship to the Father, and continues to intercede for the salvation of the world *at every single moment*. The liturgy is the continuation in every corner of time and space of Christ's own prayer and self-offering to the Father. Somewhere in the world, someone—whether a hermit in the mountains, a parish priest, a bishop in a packed cathedral, or a community of nuns in a desert convent—is always engaged in liturgical prayer. The Church's liturgy fulfills the Old Testament prophecy:

> For from the rising of the sun to its setting
> my name is great among the nations,
> and in every place incense is offered to my name,
> and is a pure offering;
> for my name is great among the nations,
> says the Lord of hosts. (Malachi 1:11)

The center of all liturgical prayer is the Mass—which, in fact, is the most perfect prayer that the earth has ever known. The rest of the liturgy flows from and points back to the Mass. The holy sacrifice of the Mass, the celebration of the

Eucharist, is the hour when time—past, present, and future—and eternity touch. Unfortunately, our experience doesn't always reflect this amazing and mysterious reality of the Mass. So let's take some time to reflect on it.

FIVE

Getting More Out of Mass

We might have the impression that the requirement to attend Mass every Sunday and holy day of obligation is arbitrary, as if the Church were on some kind of meaningless power trip, trying to control our lives and keep us in line. Nothing could be further from the truth. Mass is the anchor of our spiritual and moral life. It holds everything else in place. If we let that anchor hang loose, sooner or later the rest of our lives will drift off course, dragged away by the powerful currents of selfishness and temptation.

The Mass, the center of the liturgy, is our anchor because it is objective contact with God, and we need contact with God to find fulfillment in life. Other ways of encountering God (such as personal prayer) are helpful too, and even necessary, but cut off from the Mass they lose their objectivity. Often they depend on feelings or other external factors. If we go to a praise and worship gathering and feel good, we think we had contact with God. If we go to a praise and worship gathering and feel bad, we wonder. When we make time for personal prayer, we sometimes get distracted (we'll talk about that later), or even fall asleep, or feel as if we run out of things to say. When that happens, we can feel unsure

61

of ourselves, uncertain whether we are really praying as we should.

This doesn't mean that we shouldn't participate in these kinds of activities; it just emphasizes our need for an objective way of approaching God, a way that doesn't depend primarily on our own efforts, ideas, or feelings. That's a key role of liturgical prayer, the center of which is the Mass. Mass is the perfect act of worship, the perfect prayer—objectively perfect, because the Mass is Jesus Christ's own prayer, his own sacrifice, his own act of worship, truly made present for us—whether or not we happen to feel any spiritual warm fuzzies.

GOD'S GUARANTEE

The priest who celebrates the Mass has been configured to Christ in the very depths of his being through the sacrament of holy orders. God has set him aside to act in Christ's place, just so we can be sure that this act of worship is truly Christ's own. When we participate prayerfully in Mass, following with our minds and hearts the words, gestures, and rhythms of this simple, ancient, beautiful ritual, we are plugging into Christ's own prayer and self-offering to the Father. That's why only an ordained priest can celebrate Mass—it's part of God's guarantee.

And the prayers, readings, and rubrics of the Mass as developed and proclaimed by the Church through the centuries, under the Holy Spirit's gentle but sure guidance, are equally objective: They accurately express the truths of the faith and the sentiments of Christ himself, and so they are objectively pleasing to God. They hit the nail right on the head every time. So even if the priest is careless and sloppy, and even if the church building is ugly, and even if the music is horrid, and even if the congregation is motley—even so, when we participate in Mass, our weak and imperfect efforts to serve God are swept right up into Christ's perfect service.

Every Mass is a wrinkle in time. In the Mass, Jesus opens a corridor through history, linking three things: the here and now of our normal, everyday lives, which is always utterly unique; the historical sacrifice of his own body and blood on the cross at Calvary, which happened "once for all" at a particular place and time in history (see Hebrews 10:10); and his everlasting self-offering as it continues now in heaven (see Romans 8:34). At Mass we plug into eternity.

DOUBLE-BARRELED

The Mass consists of two basic parts: the Liturgy of the Word and the Liturgy of the Eucharist. This fundamental structure has never changed throughout the two-thousand-year history of the Church. And it traces its roots back even further, to the liturgical traditions of ancient Israel.

In the Liturgy of the Word, the sacred ministers proclaim and explain the deeds and words of God as recorded in the inspired text of the Bible. By listening attentively, we take our places beside the apostles, who spent three years living with Jesus, observing his actions and listening to his teaching in order to fill their souls with his truth. We tune our minds back in to God's wavelength, to remind us of his plans for the world and for our own lives, to stir up our appreciation for his mercy and goodness. In the Liturgy of the Word we listen to God's Word, we listen to Christ—at least, we're *supposed* to be listening.

In the Liturgy of the Eucharist, we *respond* to that Word. The word *eucharist* means "thanksgiving." And thanksgiving is the most proper response to God's mercy and goodness. But on our own, we cannot thank God properly; he deserves much more than we can give. So Christ comes to our aid. He is our "great high priest" (Hebrews 4:14), our unique "mediator" between heaven and earth (1 Timothy 2:5), exercising this mediation through his ordained minister.

And so, through the words and actions of the Catholic priest, Christ himself sacramentally *re-presents*, really makes present again, the perfect offering he made once for all on Calvary, the perfect yes he said to his Father during every moment of his earthly life in order to atone for every sinful no of humanity. The sentiments of Christ's heart are re-presented through the words of the Eucharistic prayer. The complete sacrifice of his obedience is re-presented through the offering of the bread and wine, which he turns into his very own body and blood without removing the appearances of bread and wine (a miraculous phenomenon called "transubstantiation").

The more attentively we unite our own hearts and minds to this Liturgy of the Eucharist, therefore, the more fully our lives are joined to Christ's.

That in itself—hearing God's own words in the Liturgy of the Word and participating directly in Christ's own sacrifice through the Liturgy of the Eucharist—is a miracle beyond description. All the other prayers and sacrifices of the whole human race throughout all time, all its efforts to atone for sin, to praise its Creator, to ask for his favors—including using human and animal sacrifices, cannibalism, and other strange and even grotesque rituals—all of them together are less than a grain of sand compared to a mountain when juxtaposed with a single celebration of the Eucharist.

REAL CLOSE

But it doesn't stop there. God wants to come *even closer* to us. He knows how difficult it is for us to participate with due reverence and attention in the Liturgy of the Word and the Liturgy of the Eucharist, especially when the music is bad or the congregation is noisy and distracted, or the priest is in a rush. And so, to make sure this encounter with him is as intimate and real as possible, he offers himself to us truly and sacramentally—Body, Blood, Soul, and Divinity—in Holy Communion. Under the humble appearances of bread and wine, God, the Creator and sustainer of the entire universe—daisies, whales, volcanoes, supernovas, and black holes included—comes within us and unites himself to us, becoming our very food. In the Mass it's no longer just a symbol, merely bread and wine, as it was in the Old Testament. In Holy Communion, we really receive God as the intimate companion and spiritual nourishment of our lives.

This, then, is the Mass. Through the objective, guaranteed ministry of the priest, God speaks and we respond—and that heart-to-heart conversation culminates in the intimate, unutterable embrace of Holy Communion, an embrace that happens objectively, no matter what kind of mood you're in, or how tired you are, or how distracted you may be.

THANKS, MOM

We need God; our souls yearn for him. But in this fallen world, it is often hard to find him. It's even hard to remember to look for him. And so the Church commands us to attend Mass every Sunday and every holy day; in fact, it is a grave sin to miss Sunday Mass except for a serious reason (such as sickness). We receive no such command about the other forms of personal and communal prayer; regarding those, the Church only offers constant and energetic recommendations. But Sunday Mass is a Church commandment, given with all the authority of God himself.

The Church is a good mother; she knows that sometimes children won't do what's best for them unless they're ordered to, so she orders us to attend Mass. As we grow out of spiritual infancy, however, we don't need to be ordered; we want to go. We yearn to receive God's grace and to plug every aspect of our lives into him, and we know that there's no better way to do so than by participating in Mass.

And if there is ever a time in our lives when we start skipping Mass because we don't have time or we don't feel like going, it is a sure sign that something's wrong, that our souls are sick, that our anchors are coming loose. And that can happen easily—especially if we are not developing and growing in our personal prayer lives.

Besides being essential for growing in our relationship with God, developing the spiritual discipline of daily vocal and mental prayer is also the best way to improve the quality of our participation at Mass. If Mass is boring for you, if you dread going, if you simply can't stand it, I would be willing to bet that your personal prayer life has been malnourished in some way. Other causes may also be at work, but when we fail to spend time alone with the Lord to get to know him and give him a chance to speak to our hearts, it limits our capacity to humbly enter into the mysterious and amazing drama of liturgical prayer.

Our Mass attendance—its frequency and its quality—is the most objective vital sign of our spiritual life, and our spiritual life is the key to the rest of our life. Becoming a partner in a law firm or winning an Olympic gold medal or making a million dollars may not require a vibrant relationship with God, but lasting happiness does. And, in any case, neither law firms nor gold medals nor bank accounts can buy real estate in heaven.

SIX
Warnings and Shortcuts

We have seen a lot so far.

We know why we should pray: Prayer provides the necessary soil for the life of grace—the only life that will give us lasting fulfillment—to grow and flourish in our souls.

We know what prayer is: a mysterious gift of a vital and personal relationship with the living and true God, cultivated by ongoing communication with him.

And we know the three basic forms of prayer, which we can engage in personally or communally: *vocal prayer*, in which we use and make our own the ready-made prayers of other people; *mental prayer*, in which we quietly and humbly listen to God and respond to him with thoughts and words flowing from our own hearts; and *liturgical prayer*, centered around the Mass, in which we join our voice and our intentions to the voice and intentions of the entire mystical body of Christ, along with the head of that body, Jesus himself.

We've covered a lot of ground. But I would be remiss if I failed to mention two other items. You have to be forewarned about the most common difficulties encountered as you try to jump-start and develop your prayer life. And someone needs to tell you about the shortcuts. Neither of these items is complicated, but they can make a big difference. It's somewhat like having the right-size screwdriver on hand: If you have it, the job is pretty easy; if you don't, even the small jobs become impossible.

BEATING LAZINESS

The single most common obstacle to getting our prayer life in shape is laziness. The traditional term for laziness in regard to healthy spiritual activities is *sloth*, otherwise known as one of the seven capital sins. Laziness as it relates to our prayer life shows up in two basic guises.

Before we pray, it manifests as procrastination. We can always find an excuse for praying later or for initiating a daily prayer time next week or for going on a spiritual retreat next year. When these thoughts pop up in your mind, call them what they are—lazy excuses not to pray—and tell them to go away.

The best weapon against this kind of laziness is to preempt it by making concrete, realistic prayer commitments. If we leave our prayer life entirely up to spontaneous inspiration, we will never make progress. A little bit of discipline in this area of our lives, as in almost every other area, makes a big difference.

During times of prayer, laziness enters the picture when we feel tired or drowsy, or when we simply don't feel in the mood to pray. This tempts us to cut our commitments short or simply stop trying. By giving in to this temptation, we fail to advance beyond spiritual adolescence. We get stuck in the moody-teenager stage and forfeit the joys and discoveries that come from learning how to govern our decisions by true convictions instead of by fleeting fancies and feelings.

Your antidote for this temptation is to think ahead and give a simple structure to your time of personal prayer. The structure isn't the essence of your prayer, and it doesn't have to prevent you from following unanticipated inspirations of the Holy Spirit—you can deviate from it when it seems right and helpful to do so. But if you go into a time of personal prayer without any structure at all, you may become like a lazy autumn leaf blowing wherever the gusty winds want to take you.

It's important to remember that overcoming laziness isn't just a question of trying harder. It doesn't depend only on our efforts. The roots of spiritual laziness, of sloth, go deep. When we pray sincerely, we open ourselves up to hear what God is asking us, and he may be asking us to do something uncomfortable, to follow a path that requires self-denial, to make a change in a relationship or a habit or lifestyle choice, or to repent from a sin. Subconsciously, sloth often finds its roots in a self-centered attachment to our own will and preferences, traditionally called "pride," another capital sin. That kind of unhealthy pride makes us allergic to prayer. But do not be afraid! The allergy wanes as our prayer life waxes.

DEALING WITH DISTRACTIONS

When we pray, whether it's personal or communal prayer, vocal or mental or liturgical, distractions happen. Our mind wanders. This is the most normal thing in the world, for one simple reason.

You see, our relationship with God, the essential core of our prayer life, is different from any other relationship. Instead of happening directly, it is mediated by faith. When I call my sister on the phone or have a video call with my boss, we hear each other's voices and, in the case of video, see each other's faces. When I get a cup of coffee with a friend or go out for a beer with a buddy, it's the same thing. But when I turn my attention to the Lord, I don't normally hear his voice with my ears; I don't usually see his face with my eyes; I can't shake his hand or give him a pat on the back.

Some people use this as an excuse to claim that God is not real. That's an illogical argument we don't need to address here. The truth is, God is more real than anything or anyone else. His mode of being is far superior to ours; it's on a different level. And that's why our relationship with him unfolds here on earth through faith, through *mediated contact* with him and not through *immediate* contact with him. When I address myself to God, I know that he hears me, but I know it because of my faith, not because I see him turn his head and look at me. When he touches my heart with a phrase from the Bible or a moving glimpse of natural beauty, I recognize his presence and action by faith, not by sight: "for we walk by faith, not by sight" (2 Corinthians 5:7).

Our faith doesn't contradict reason. In fact, when we look at the whole worldview offered by Christianity, and when we look at the entire history of how the Church has impacted the world through her members who have lived their faith most authentically, our faith appears immensely, wonderfully reasonable. But it can't be reduced to mathematical formulas and test-tubeable substances. In fact, not even natural human relationships can be so reduced, let alone the amazing, supernatural relationship that we have with God.

Because we encounter God through the mediation of faith, distractions are a perennial bugbear. Our five external senses and two internal senses (imagination and memory) tend to get tugged at and whisked away by any physical or physiological stimulus they come into contact with. That's how they are made. So we have to educate them. We have to train them not to interfere with our conversation with God, whether vocal, mental, or liturgical, but to contribute to it.

This training takes two forms. First, we can engage our senses in our prayer: using holy images, candles, and incense and choosing wisely where we go to pray (a place more conducive to our faith-filled encounter with God than to the hustle and bustle of other stuff), for example. Second, we can stay calm when distractions batter our minds and bombard our times of prayer. Stay calm, and as soon as you realize that you are distracted, simply identify the distraction, then dismiss it—whether that means making a quick note (if the distraction is something like "Don't forget to send in that RSVP!") or just turning your attention back to God, like gently steering your car back onto the road after your tires hit a rumble strip on the shoulder of the highway. And if you have to do this every minute, or ten times a minute, don't worry. Every time you do, you are winning a victory of faith, exercising your faith, and making your faith grow. If you persevere, distractions will gradually be less and less of a factor in your prayer life.

THE MOST IMPORTANT FIFTEEN MINUTES OF YOUR LIFE: YOUR DAILY GOD TIME

There are other obstacles to daily prayer, but sloth and distraction are the most common and the ones you need to be aware of right now. Don't let yourself be discouraged by them. You are never alone in your battle against them. God himself is on your side! "If God is for us, who is against us?" (Romans 8:31).

By now you have surely realized that the shortest path to jump-starting and developing your prayer life is committing yourself to a daily God time that includes mental prayer. Maybe you used to do this. Maybe you have never done this. Maybe you do this sometimes. If you want to experience more fully and intensely the fruits and gifts of the Holy Spirit, you need to decide firmly to make it a reality in your life. God will do the rest, but even he cannot do this for you. You need to make the decision.

A daily God time is the only way to make everything that we have seen throughout the book into a reality for you. Once you make the decision, you may find it hard to follow through. Don't worry. Renew your commitment as many times as you need to. Gradually, your daily God time will begin to take its unique shape, and you will start to experience the transformation in grace that only a growing prayer life brings.

Choose a good time, a good place (in accordance with everything we have already discussed), and a structure that is attractive to you. Start with at least fifteen minutes, stick to it for a month, and then make adjustments. Here are some ideas for a structure (choose one or two from each section):

What to begin with (two to three minutes—these are ways to do the Concentrate step of mental prayer)
- Listen to a favorite faith-based piece of music that can help you enter into God's presence.

- Pray a decade of the Rosary (if you are familiar with this prayer and like it).
- Pray your favorite psalm or other vocal prayer.
- Use an abbreviated form of Morning or Evening Prayer from the Liturgy of the Hours.
- Write down in a prayer journal three things from the past twenty-four hours you are grateful for, thanking God for them.

What to do next (five to ten minutes—this corresponds to the Consider and Converse steps)

- Read and reflect on a passage from the Bible.
- Read and reflect on a good spiritual book meant for Christian meditation.
- Read and reflect on the readings for daily Mass.
- Gaze prayerfully at a beautiful image of Christian art or a compelling scene from nature.

How to finish (one to three minutes)

- Pray a favorite vocal prayer.
- Write down a resolution or a commitment that flows from your time with God.
- Write a note to God in your prayer journal.
- Ask God to help and bless you and the people in your life whom you love and who are in need.
- Light a candle that will keep burning (near a holy image in your parish Church or adoration chapel, for example) while you continue with your day, as a sign of the love God has for you and the love you have for him.

- Take a phrase that really resonated with you and write it down somewhere you will be able to see it throughout the day.
- Make the Sign of the Cross.

You can do it. You've got this. If you try it for a month, I guarantee there is absolutely no way in the universe you will regret it.

THREE SHORTCUTS

Finally, I want to share some of the practical wisdom that has come down to us throughout the centuries. Growing in prayer involves effort and battle, not just because of sloth and distractions but also because we have spiritual enemies (the devil and his minions) who work very hard to slow down or even destroy our relationship with God. So it's helpful to know about three useful shortcuts to growth in prayer. They aren't substitutes for daily God time, but they help make it easier and more fruitful.

Spiritual Reading

First, take some time every week for what tradition calls "spiritual reading." This kind of reading continues to educate you in the faith. Through it, you grow in your understanding of what God has revealed to us about himself, our world, and his plan for our lives. You can read good spiritual books, lives of the saints, writings by the saints themselves, biographies and testimonies, and so on. Nowadays, you can even do this spiritual "reading" through listening to good Catholic radio shows or podcasts—there are so many!

The point here is to fill your mind, your thoughts, and your imagination with good, solid Christian ideas—this, obviously, helps fertilize the soil of prayer. If we don't do this, the noisy and less nourishing (if not poisonous) ideas of our increasingly secularized culture will dominate our interior space. That makes it harder to pray. You don't have to do this every day—though it would be great if you could. But even once or twice a week will make a tangible impact.

Make Room for Silence

Second, build some silence into your life. Our digitized world is noisier than in any other period of human history. Audible noise, visual noise, psychological noise, commercial noise—we are constantly bombarded by voices that are aggressively competing for our attention. Turn them off occasionally. Allow yourself to be in silence sometimes. Learn to savor one or two helpings of silence every day.

Maybe it's just a matter of taking five or ten minutes during your commute without listening to anything or talking to anyone. Maybe it's just a matter of going off-line one day a week (Sunday, the Lord's Day, would be a good choice). Maybe it's just a matter of drinking a cup of tea on the back porch after dinner and watching the sunset.

Whatever it may mean for you, try it. See what happens. Silence, for our spiritual life, is like the space inside the body of a violin: It is what allows the music to resonate. Fill that space with sand, and not even the greatest violinist can produce so much as a squeak. Take some of the sand out of your life, so that God's voice can resound better within you.

Reconnect with Nature

Finally, get back in tune with nature. I don't mean become a hippie and start hugging trees. I just mean that this beautiful, amazing earth is God's creation, and he created it *for us*. We can get to know the hearts and minds of great artists by taking time to appreciate their paintings and sculptures. In the same way, and even more so, we can get to know our God and heavenly Father by taking time to appreciate the beauty of his creations.

Going for a walk in the woods, taking a run through the park, sitting by the lake and feeding the ducks, standing on the beach and feeling the sand between your toes and the invigorating sting of the salty breeze, making a small garden (if you have the time), even just admiring the colors and textures of the vegetables you eat in your salads—how much delight and glory you can give God by granting yourself permission to enjoy these gifts of his! Doing so helps you learn to recognize his voice in your heart more and more easily, and nothing enhances your prayer life more than that.

LET THE ADVENTURE BEGIN

I hope this practical discussion of why we pray, what prayer is, and how to pray has helped open up a new horizon for you, or maybe refreshed some dormant desires. God's grace is present in your life. He wants that spiritual acorn to take root and grow and lead you to a life overflowing with the fruits of the Holy Spirit—love, joy, peace, patience, kindness, goodness, gentleness, and self-control—and humming with the gifts of that same Spirit: wisdom, understanding, knowledge, piety, fear of the Lord, fortitude, and counsel. That's the path to meaning and the deep, lasting fulfillment that you yearn for, that we all yearn for. That's the only path, the path of prayer, of courageously engaging in and developing a vital and personal relationship with the living and true God.

You are not alone in this adventure. God is at your side and already guiding you. You just have to keep taking each next step, one at a time. He will take care of the rest. As St. James put it: "Draw near to God and he will draw near to you" (James 4:8).

Now you know how to provide the seed of grace with the soil it needs to grow and flourish. You don't need to wait to get started. You don't need to worry about "doing it right." You just need to step out in faith and trust in the God who created you, knows you through and through, and will never be able to love you more or less than he does now, because he is already all in for you. Let's let him have the last word:

> Fear not, for I have redeemed you;
> I have called you by name, you are mine. . . .
> Can a woman forget her sucking child,
> that she should have no compassion on the son of
>   her womb?
> Even these may forget,
> yet I will never forget you.
> Behold, I have graven you on the palms of my hands . . .
> (Isaiah 43:1; 49:15–16)

ABOUT THE AUTHOR

Fr. John Bartunek, LC, SThD, received his BA in History from Stanford University in 1990. He comes from an evangelical Christian background and became a member of the Catholic Church in 1991. He is the author of *The Better Part* and several other books. Fr. John currently splits his time between Michigan, where he continues his writing apostolate and serves as a confessor and spiritual director at the Queen of the Family Retreat Center, and Rome, where he teaches theology at Regina Apostolorum. His online do-it-yourself retreats are available at RCSpirituality.org, and he answers questions about the spiritual life at SpiritualDirection.com.

NOTES

NOTES

NOTES

NOTES

HAVE YOU EVER WONDERED HOW THE CATHOLIC FAITH COULD HELP YOU LIVE BETTER?

How it could help you find more *joy* at work, *manage* your personal finances, *improve* your marriage, or make you a *better* parent?

THERE IS GENIUS IN CATHOLICISM.

When *Catholicism* is lived as it is intended to be, it elevates every part of our lives. It may sound simple, but they say *genius is taking something complex and making it simple.*

Dynamic Catholic started with a dream: to help ordinary people discover the *genius of Catholicism.*

Wherever you are in your journey, we want to meet you there and walk with you, *step by step*, helping you to discover God and become *the-best-version-of-yourself.*

To find more helpful resources, visit us online at DynamicCatholic.com.

▊ Dynamic Catholic

FEED YOUR SOUL.